SKY WATCHING

Earth's Atmosphere

Carmel Reilly

Marshall Cavendish
Benchmark
New York

This edition first published in 2012 in the United States of America by
Marshall Cavendish Benchmark
An imprint of Marshall Cavendish Corporation

Website: www.marshallcavendish.us

This publication represents the opinions and views of the author based on Carmel Reilly's personal experience, knowledge, and research. The information in this book serves as a general guide only. The author and publisher have used their best efforts in preparing this book and disclaim liability rising directly and indirectly from the use and application of this book.

Other Marshall Cavendish Offices: Marshall Cavendish International (Asia) Private Limited, 1 New Industrial Road, Singapore 536196 • Marshall Cavendish International (Thailand) Co Ltd. 253 Asoke, 12th Flr, Sukhumvit 21 Road, Klongtoey Nua, Wattana, Bangkok 10110, Thailand • Marshall Cavendish (Malaysia) Sdn Bhd, Times Subang, Lot 46, Subang Hi-Tech Industrial Park, Batu Tiga, 40000 Shah Alam, Selangor Darul Ehsan, Malaysia

Marshall Cavendish is a trademark of Times Publishing Limited

All websites were available and accurate when this book was sent to press.

Library of Congress Cataloging-in-Publication Data

Reilly, Carmel, 1957-
  Earth's atmosphere / Carmel Reilly.
    p. cm. — (Sky watching)
  Summary: "Provides scientific information about Earth's atmosphere"—Provided by publisher.
  Includes index.
  ISBN 978-1-60870-580-1
  1. Atmosphere—Juvenile literature. I. Title.
  QC863.5.R45 2012
  551.5—dc22
                        2010044015

Publisher: Carmel Heron
Commissioning Editor: Niki Horin
Managing Editor: Vanessa Lanaway
Project Editor: Tim Clarke
Editor: Paige Amor
Proofreader: Helena Newton
Designer: Polar Design
Page layout: Romy Pearse
Photo Researcher: Legendimages
Illustrator: Adrian Hogan
Production Controller: Vanessa Johnson

Printed in China

Acknowledgments
The author and publisher are grateful to the following for permission to reproduce copyright material:

Front cover photograph: Aurora borealis in night sky over lake © Shutterstock/Pi-Lens.

Photographs courtesy of: Corbis/Image Source, **11**; Dreamstime.com/Budda, **20**, /Bvladimir, **8**, /Carrieanne, **28**, /Lcwoodward, **13**, /Romko, **14**; iStockphoto/Pierre Landry, **12**, /Rtimages, **17**, /Mike Sonnenberg, **5** (bottom), /Sergii Tsololo, border element throughout; NASA/Goddard Space Flight Center Scientific Visualization Studio, Greg Shirah, **29**, /Lewis Research Center, **15**, /Lunar and Planetary Laboratory, **5** (top); Photolibrary/Alain Even, **19**; Shutterstock/Pi-Lens, **1**.

While every care has been taken to trace and acknowledge copyright, the publisher tenders their apologies for any accidental infringement where copyright has proved untraceable. They would be pleased to come to a suitable arrangement with the rightful owner in each case.

Please Note
At the time of printing, the Internet addresses appearing in this book were correct. Owing to the dynamic nature of the Internet, however, we cannot guarantee that all these addresses will remain correct.

Contents

Glossary Words
Words that are printed in **bold** are explained in the glossary on page 31.

What Does It Mean?
Words that are within a **box** are explained in the "What Does It Mean?" panel at the bottom of the page.

SKY WATCHING

When we sky watch, we look at everything above Earth. This includes what is in Earth's **atmosphere** and the objects we can see beyond it, in space .

Why Do We Sky Watch?

Sky watching helps us understand more about Earth's place in space. Earth is our home. It is also a planet that is part of a space neighborhood called the **solar system**. When we sky watch, we learn more about Earth and our neighbors both inside and outside the solar system.

What Objects Are in the Sky?

There are thousands of objects in the sky above Earth. These are Earth's neighbors— the Sun, the Moon, planets, stars, and flying space rocks (**comets, asteroids,** and **meteoroids**). Some can be seen at night and others can be seen during the day. Although some are visible with the human eye, all objects must be viewed through a telescope to be seen more clearly.

When and How Can We See Objects in the Sky?

Object in the Sky	Visible with Only the Human Eye	Visible Only through a Telescope	Visible during the Day	Visible at Night
Earth's Atmosphere	✗	✗	✗	✗
Sun	✓ (Do not view directly)	✗ (View only with a special telescope)	✓	✗
Moon	✓	✗	Sometimes	✓
Planets	Sometimes	Sometimes	Sometimes	✓
Stars	Sometimes	Sometimes	✗	✓
Comets	Sometimes	Sometimes	✗	✓
Asteroids	Sometimes	Sometimes	✗	✓
Meteoroids	Sometimes	Sometimes	✗	✓

WHAT DOES IT MEAN?

space The area in which the solar system, stars, and galaxies exist, also known as the universe.

EARTH'S ATMOSPHERE

The atmosphere around Earth is invisible. However, we can see **matter**, such as dust and water, in the atmosphere. We can also feel the temperature and movement of the air.

Watching the Atmosphere

People have always watched the skies. Only 300 years ago, scientists discovered that the air around them and the skies just above were all part of the atmosphere. Thanks to more discoveries, we now know what the atmosphere is made of, what kind of matter and objects exist in it, and what it does for Earth.

Λ Sky watching can be done during the day or night, with or without a telescope. Just look up!

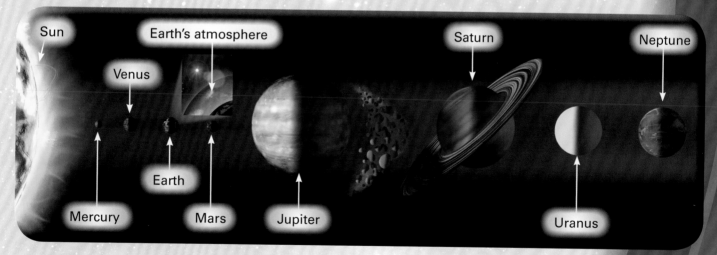

Sun Earth's atmosphere Saturn Neptune

Venus

Mercury Earth Mars Jupiter Uranus

Λ The Earth's atmosphere is the area that lies between Earth and space. This diagram shows the approximate relative sizes of the Sun and the planets. The distances between them are not to scale.

WHAT IS EARTH'S ATMOSPHERE?

The atmosphere is made up of layers of **gases** that surround Earth. The atmosphere formed billions of years ago. It acts like a blanket that protects Earth from the dangers of space. The atmosphere helps to create the right conditions to sustain life.

The Atmosphere Is Earth's Blanket

The atmosphere is made up of five layers of gases that stretch more than 311 miles (500 kilometers) into space. Theses layers act like a blanket wrapped around Earth. They keep the planet warm and protect it from the Sun's strong rays. Conditions within the atmosphere provide the air and water that allows life to exist on Earth.

V Earth's atmosphere acts as a blanket, and protects the planet from the harsh Sun and from many collisions with space rocks.

Distance to nearest space object (the Moon): 238,855 miles (384,400 km)

Atmosphere Fact

The word "atmosphere" comes from two ancient words. The Greek word *atmos*, which means vapor, or mist, and the Latin word *sphaera*, which means sphere, or ball.

Depth of the atmosphere: 311 to 621 mi. (500–1,000 km) above Earth

Earth

The Atmosphere Was Formed Billions of Years Ago

The atmosphere was first formed about 3.8 billion years ago. It was made by gases that were given off by volcanoes on Earth's surface. About 2.7 billion years ago, the first plants began to grow on Earth. They produced a gas called oxygen . Oxygen mixed with the other gases to make air.

Between 3 billion to 4 billion years ago, volcanoes gave off gases that formed an atmosphere around Earth.

Between 1 billion to 2 billion years ago, plant life began to grow and give off oxygen.

When oxygen was added to the atmosphere, it made the air breathable for animals and people.

FAMOUS SKY WATCHERS

In 1774 Carl Wilhelm Scheele, a Swedish chemist, discovered the gas we know as oxygen in the air. He called it "fire air." In 1777 Antoine Lavoisier, a French chemist, gave it the name oxygen.

WHAT DOES IT MEAN

oxygen An invisible gas produced by plants that makes up about 20 percent of the Earth's atmosphere and makes air breathable.

WHAT DOES EARTH'S ATMOSPHERE LOOK LIKE?

From Earth, the atmosphere, which includes the air around us, is invisible. However, we can see matter and objects in the atmosphere, and we see the daytime sky as blue.

The Atmosphere Is Invisible, But ...

Although the gases in the atmosphere are invisible, water vapor , smoke, and dust carried in the air are visible. We can see clouds and weather activity, such as rain, snow, and lightning, in the atmosphere. We can also see and feel the effects of wind, and feel the temperature of the air.

V Wind, temperature, and clouds are all part of weather activity that happens in the atmosphere and affects Earth.

Atmosphere Fact

Scientists use balloons to find out about the atmosphere. They have equipment that can measure wind speed and temperature, and take samples of the different parts of the atmosphere. This helps them to understand what elements make up the atmosphere.

Clouds are made up of water vapor.

Temperature affects all life on Earth.

Wind affects trees, plants, and people.

WHAT DOES IT MEAN ? water vapor Tiny particles of water that are no longer a liquid and can be carried in the air.

The Atmosphere Makes the Sky Look Blue

If we were in space, the sky would look black during the day. On Earth, the sky looks blue. This is because of Earth's atmosphere.

The Atmosphere Scatters Blue Light

The Sun's light seems white, but it is really made up of every color. When this light shines on Earth, most colors reach the surface without stopping. However, blue light has a short **wavelength** that causes it to bump into **particles** in the atmosphere. When the blue light hits these particles, it scatters in different directions rather than going straight to Earth's surface. The sky looks blue because when we look up we see that all of the blue light has been scattered.

Light from the Sun is made up of every color.

When the Sun's light hits the particles in the atmosphere, a lot of the blue light is scattered.

Other colors reach Earth's surface.

The scattering of blue light in Earth's atmosphere is called Rayleigh scattering.

What Is Earth's Atmosphere Made of?

The atmosphere is divided into five layers, called the troposphere, the stratosphere, the mesosphere, the thermosphere, and the exosphere. The same gases are found in all layers of the atmosphere. However, the air becomes thinner in each layer and the temperature in each layer is different. Dust, smoke, and water vapor are also found in the lower layers of the atmosphere.

Exosphere Temperature range: 1,832°F (1,000°C) and above	Contains a tiny amount of the atmosphere's gases
Thermosphere Temperature range: −148°F to 2,732°F (−100°C to 1,500°C)	Contains very little of the atmosphere's gases
Mesosphere Temperature range: 32°F to −148°F (0°C to −100°C)	Contains less than 5% of the atmosphere's gases
Stratosphere Temperature range: −58°F to 32°F (−50°C to 0°C)	Contains about 20% of the atmosphere's gases
Troposphere Temperature range: −58°F to 77°F (−50°C to 25°C)	Contains about 75% of the atmosphere's gases

 As the atmosphere stretches upward, the gases in the air become thinner until they finally fade away into space.

FAMOUS SKY WATCHERS

French meteorologist Leon Teisserenc de Bort was the first person to realize that the atmosphere contained more than one layer. He gave the troposphere and the stratosphere their names.

The Lowest Layer Is the Troposphere

The troposphere starts at Earth's surface and travels upward for about 7.5 mi. (12 km). Although it is the narrowest layer of the atmosphere, it contains about 75 percent of all the atmosphere's gases. It also contains large amounts of water and dust. The troposphere is the only layer of atmosphere in which weather occurs.

Rain, sunshine, wind, and clouds all occur in the troposphere.

11

The Second Layer Is the Stratosphere

The stratosphere starts at the top of the troposphere and rises to 31 mi. (50 km) above Earth's surface. It contains about 20 percent of the gases in the atmosphere. It has less water vapor and less air movement than the troposphere.

FAMOUS SKY WATCHERS

In 1913, French scientists Charles Fabry and Henri Buisson discovered an important band of gas within the stratosphere called the **ozone layer**. This layer of gas absorbs many of the Sun's harmful **ultraviolet (UV) rays** and stops them from reaching Earth's surface.

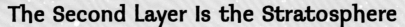
Jets and other aircraft often fly in the stratosphere to avoid the weather conditions of the troposphere below.

The Third Layer Is the Mesosphere

The mesosphere is the next layer of atmosphere above the stratosphere. It lies between 31 and 50 mi. (50 and 80 km) above Earth. The mesosphere is the coldest layer of the atmosphere, with temperatures dropping as low as −148°F (−100°C). Icy clouds, called noctilucent clouds, sometimes form in this layer.

Atmosphere Fact

The air in the mesosphere is thin compared to the lower layers. However, it is still thick enough to slow down and burn up small space objects, such as meteoroids, when they enter the atmosphere.

Noctilucent clouds are also called "night shining" clouds. They can be seen in the sky from some parts of Earth in the summer.

The Fourth Layer Is the Thermosphere

The thermosphere is the fourth layer of the atmosphere. It reaches about 311 mi. (500 km) above Earth. The air in the thermosphere is quite thin. It is also very hot because it absorbs UV rays from the Sun. Temperatures in the thermosphere are as high as 2,732°F (1,500°C).

V The aurora borealis is also called the northern lights. It is seen in the thermosphere above the Arctic Ocean.

FAMOUS SKY WATCHERS

For centuries, many people have tried to explain auroras, the colorful light shows seen from Earth, near the North and South Poles. In the late 1800s, Norwegian scientist Kristian Birkeland discovered that auroras are caused when dust particles from space and particles in the thermosphere crash together.

The Highest Layer Is the Exosphere

The exosphere is the last and highest layer of the atmosphere. The gases of the exosphere are thin, and temperatures are quite cool. Scientists believe that the exosphere ends about 621 mi. (1,000 km) above Earth. This is where the last of the atmosphere's gases escape into space.

Atmosphere Fact

Many **satellites** that are made by people orbit Earth in the atmosphere. Some of these satellites check the weather and temperatures. Others send communications from one part of Earth to another.

The Advanced Communications Technology Satellite (ACTS) was sent into space by NASA. It orbits Earth in the exosphere, sending back information about weather conditions.

WHAT DOES IT MEAN | orbit | To travel around another, larger space object.

WHAT HAPPENS IN EARTH'S ATMOSPHERE?

From the ground, we can see that the atmosphere is a busy place. The air is always moving and the weather is always changing. A lot of bird, insect, and human activity also takes place in the atmosphere.

Air Movement in the Atmosphere Keeps Earth Warm

Air movement is started by the heat of the Sun. The Sun does not heat Earth evenly. When one part is warm, another part is cold. The heat from the warm areas rises into the atmosphere, pushing the cold air downward. This creates air movement and keeps temperatures even.

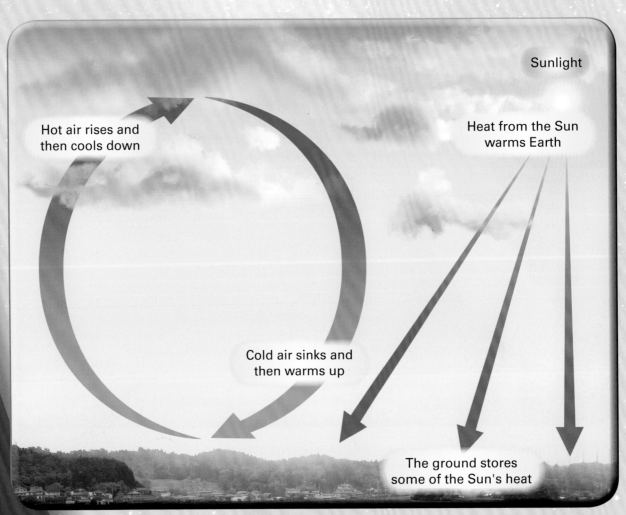

Sunlight

Hot air rises and then cools down

Heat from the Sun warms Earth

Cold air sinks and then warms up

The ground stores some of the Sun's heat

The ground stores much of the heat from the Sun and warms the air around it. This contributes to the movement of warm and cool air.

Weather Activity in the Atmosphere Changes Conditions on Earth

Weather is the word we use to talk about changing conditions in the atmosphere. Weather is created in the troposphere. It is caused by sunshine, air, and water. The meeting of hot and cold air in the atmosphere can create winds, rain, thunderstorms, and lightning.

V When the water vapor in clouds becomes heavy and cold, it is released as rain, hail, or snow.

FAMOUS SKY WATCHERS

Vilhelm Bjerknes was one of the first scientific meteorologists. In 1917 he set up a series of weather stations in Norway. Using information from these stations, he discovered a great deal about how weather was formed in the atmosphere.

Flying Animals Move through the Atmosphere

Bats, most birds, and some insects are animals that are able to fly. They use the atmosphere as a way to get from place to place. Flying animals can move around freely to hunt and eat. They are also safer from attack by animals on the ground.

V Birds are able to fly because of "lift." This creates a pressure difference between the air above and the air below their wings.

3. The pressure difference results in what is called lift.

2. As the wings flap, the air pressure created over the top of the wings is lower than the pressure created under the wings.

1. The bird thrusts forward and begins to flap its wings.

Lift

Air pressure

Thrust

Atmosphere Fact

The first animals on Earth to fly in the atmosphere were pterosaurs. They were winged reptiles that lived between 200 million and 65 million years ago, in the time of the dinosaurs.

People Move through the Atmosphere

The atmosphere is all around us. Everything we do takes place in the atmosphere. However, people have always been curious about exploring the skies above. The first human journey into the air was in a hot air balloon in 1783. The first airplane flight was in 1903. Since then, airplanes have become a common form of transportation. There are thousands in the air every day. Since the 1960s, space stations and satellites have been launched into orbit in the upper layers of the atmosphere.

More than 200 years since the first hot air balloon flight, people still enjoy exploring the skies in hot air balloons.

FAMOUS SKY WATCHERS

Aircraft are not the only human-made objects or matter in the sky. The atmosphere also carries smoke and pollution caused by human activities. Atmospheric scientists, such as those at the Environmental Protection Agency, spend their time studying air pollution and looking at ways to reduce it.

HOW DOES EARTH'S ATMOSPHERE STAY IN PLACE?

The gases in our atmosphere stay in place because of Earth's **gravity**. Earth's gravity pulls everything that is smaller than Earth toward it. Gravity pulls the atmosphere towards Earth and stops the gases from drifting off into space.

Earth's Gravity Keeps the Atmosphere in Place

The bigger an object, the stronger its **gravitational pull**. Earth is big and so it has a strong gravitational pull. The particles that make up gases are small and have very little gravitational pull. This means that the gravity of Earth has a strong pull on all the gases in its atmosphere. This keeps the gases close to Earth's surface.

FAMOUS SKY WATCHERS

British scientist Sir Isaac Newton was the first person to advance the theory of gravity. It explains why objects, and even matter such as gases, stay close to the surface of Earth.

V Compared to Earth, people are very small, which is why skydivers are pulled toward Earth after jumping from a plane.

Heavier Gases Are Pulled Closer to Earth

Some gases are heavier than others. The heaviest gases, such as oxygen, are pulled closer to the Earth's surface by gravity. This pushes many of the lighter gases higher into the atmosphere. Over time, a tiny number of these lighter gases escape Earth's gravity and drift off into space.

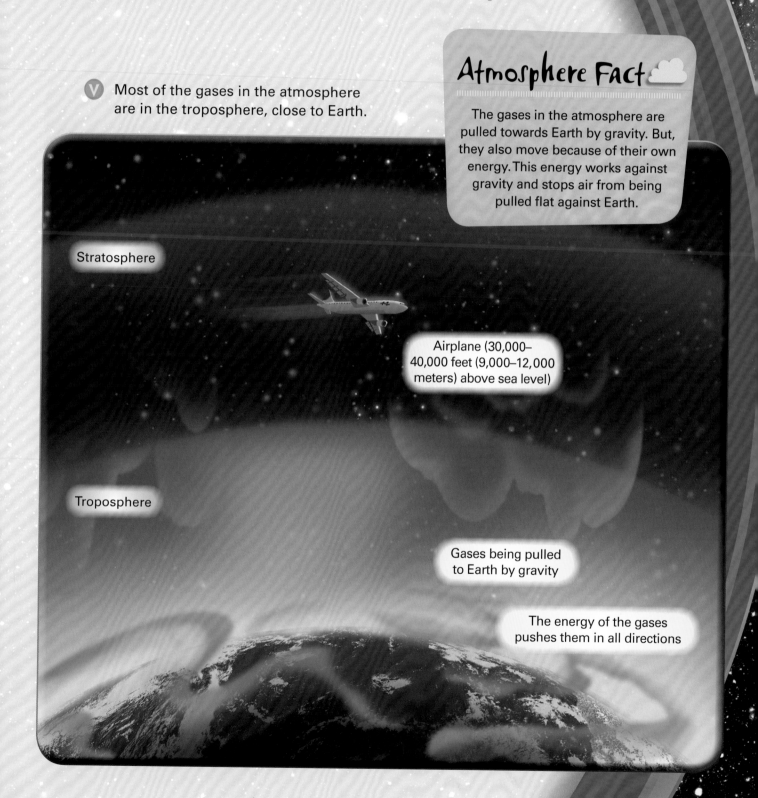

Ⓥ Most of the gases in the atmosphere are in the troposphere, close to Earth.

Atmosphere Fact

The gases in the atmosphere are pulled towards Earth by gravity. But, they also move because of their own energy. This energy works against gravity and stops air from being pulled flat against Earth.

Stratosphere

Airplane (30,000–40,000 feet (9,000–12,000 meters) above sea level)

Troposphere

Gases being pulled to Earth by gravity

The energy of the gases pushes them in all directions

WHY IS THE ATMOSPHERE IMPORTANT TO EARTH?

Without the atmosphere, we would not have life on Earth. The atmosphere protects Earth from the harmful effects of the Sun. At the same time, it uses the Sun's energy to provide the warmth, water, and air needed for life on Earth.

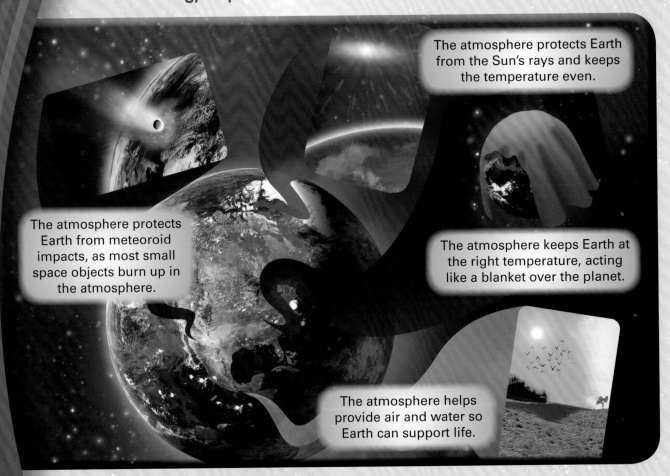

The atmosphere protects Earth from the Sun's rays and keeps the temperature even.

The atmosphere protects Earth from meteoroid impacts, as most small space objects burn up in the atmosphere.

The atmosphere keeps Earth at the right temperature, acting like a blanket over the planet.

The atmosphere helps provide air and water so Earth can support life.

⚠ The atmosphere is important to Earth in many ways.

The Atmosphere Protects Earth from Meteoroids

Meteoroids are small space objects that are made of rock and travel through space. If they pass close to Earth, they are pulled toward Earth by its gravity. However, rather than crashing to Earth, most of these objects are burned up in the atmosphere.

What If There Were No Atmosphere?

Thousands of small space objects, such as meteoroids, burn up in or are slowed by Earth's atmosphere every day. These objects travel between 12 and 43 mi. (20 and 70 km) per second! If there were no atmosphere, many of these objects would crash to Earth with great force.

The Atmosphere Protects Earth from the Sun's Rays

The Sun gives off **radiation**. Radiation is a form of energy. The Sun's radiation reaches Earth in the forms of heat and light. Although heat and light are good for Earth, some parts of the Sun's radiation can damage life on our planet. Most of the harmful radiation, such as UV rays, is filtered out by the ozone layer in the stratosphere.

What If There Were No Atmosphere?

If there were no atmosphere on Earth, more of the Sun's heat and energy would hit Earth. The levels of radiation would be so high that plants, animals, and people would not be able to survive.

Ⓥ Most of the Sun's UV rays are stopped by the atmosphere, but some still reach Earth's surface.

Atmosphere Fact

Even small amounts of UV rays are harmful to a person's skin and eyes. To be protected against its effects, you should wear sunglasses and sunscreen while out in the Sun.

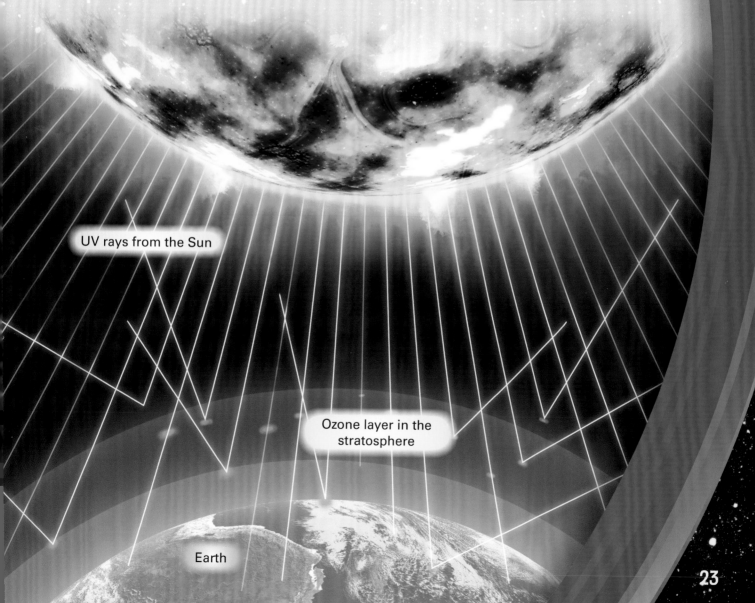

UV rays from the Sun

Ozone layer in the stratosphere

Earth

The Atmosphere Keeps Earth at the Right Temperature

The atmosphere acts like a blanket to keep Earth at the right temperature. The blanket works like a greenhouse, trapping the warmth of the Sun and keeping it from escaping back into space. Underneath the blanket, winds move warm and cold air from place to place. This keeps the temperature even around the planet.

V Air is always moving around Earth, warming cooler areas and cooling areas that are too hot.

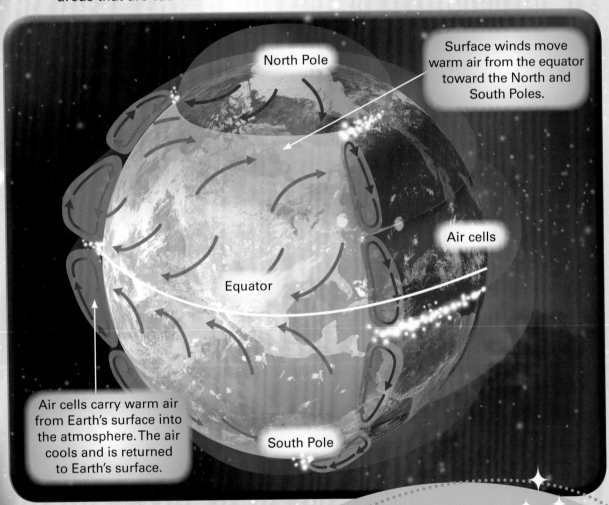

North Pole

Surface winds move warm air from the equator toward the North and South Poles.

Air cells

Equator

Air cells carry warm air from Earth's surface into the atmosphere. The air cools and is returned to Earth's surface.

South Pole

FAMOUS SKY WATCHERS

French mathematician Gustave-Gaspard de Coriolis discovered the worldwide movement of air. Air is pushed north and south from the equator, or the center of Earth. This air movement is called the Coriolis Effect.

The Greenhouse Effect Warms Earth

The greenhouse effect is a natural process in which the Sun heats up Earth and its atmosphere. The Sun's energy, or radiation, flows to Earth. Some energy is reflected from Earth and returns to space. However, most energy is stored in the Earth itself or is trapped by the atmosphere. This keeps the Earth at an even, warm temperature.

What If There Were No Atmosphere?

If there were no atmosphere, temperatures on Earth would not be even. It would be very hot during the day and very cold at night. All the energy from the Sun would escape back into space.

V The atmosphere around Earth acts like the glass in a greenhouse to keep Earth warm.

Atmosphere Fact

The atmosphere keeps Earth at an average temperature of 59°F (15°C). On the Moon, which has very little atmosphere, temperatures average 34°F (1°C).

Some radiation is reflected back out to space.

The atmosphere traps a lot of the radiation and stops it from going back into space. The radiation stays in the atmosphere and keeps it warm.

Radiation from the Sun passes through the atmosphere.

Radiation is absorbed by Earth's surface, warming it.

The Atmosphere Helps Provide Air and Water

The atmosphere carries air and water. Air is made up mostly of the gases **nitrogen** and oxygen. The oxygen and water in the atmosphere are what allows life on Earth to exist. Oxygen and water are both used and recreated in processes called the oxygen cycle and the water cycle.

Air Is Provided in the Oxygen Cycle

Oxygen is vital for life on Earth. Humans and animals need to have oxygen in the air to breathe. Oxygen is used and recreated in a process called the oxygen cycle.

People and animals breathe oxygen in and breathe **carbon dioxide** out. Plants use the energy of the Sun, water, and carbon dioxide gas (from people and animals) to grow. As they grow, they give off oxygen, which goes into the atmosphere. This process is the oxygen cycle.

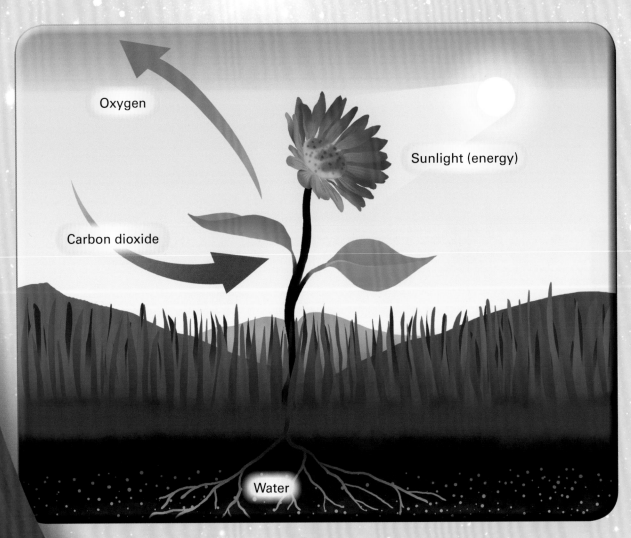

Oxygen needed by people and animals, and carbon dioxide needed by plants, are both carried in the atmosphere.

Water Is Provided in the Water Cycle

Living things need water. Water in the atmosphere is used and recreated in the water cycle.

Water stored in oceans, lakes, snow, and ice is turned into water vapor by the heat of the Sun. This rises into the atmosphere and becomes clouds. When clouds become heavy and cold they let the water out as rain, snow, hail, or fog. This is called the water cycle.

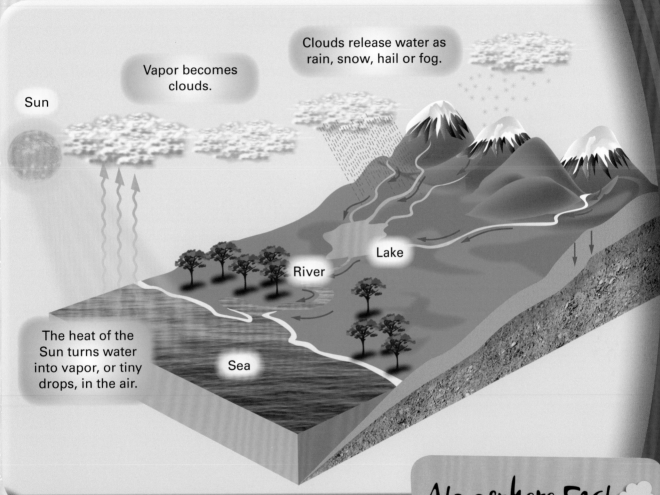

Clouds release water as rain, snow, hail or fog.

Vapor becomes clouds.

Sun

The heat of the Sun turns water into vapor, or tiny drops, in the air.

Sea

River

Lake

Ⓐ Water is always moving from the Earth's surface, into the atmosphere, and back again. This is called the water cycle.

What If There Were No Atmosphere?

If there were no atmosphere, Earth would have no air or water. Without air and water, there would be no life on Earth.

Atmosphere Fact

People need freshwater to drink. However, only 3 percent of all water in and around Earth is freshwater. The remaining 97 percent of water on Earth is found in oceans, which are saltwater.

WHAT IS THE FUTURE OF EARTH'S ATMOSPHERE?

Scientists have found that Earth's atmosphere has warmed by 33°F (0.6°C) in the last thirty years. Although this may not seem like a lot, if temperatures keep rising like this it will have a huge effect on Earth's life.

The Atmosphere Is Getting Hotter

The heating of the atmosphere is called global warming. Most scientists think global warming has been largely caused by human activities. Burning **fossil fuels** and cutting down rain forests contribute to global warming. These activities put extra carbon dioxide gases into the atmosphere. This adds to the greenhouse effect and causes Earth to heat up.

V Global warming has melted a lot of sea ice in the Arctic Ocean, reducing the habitat that animals —such as polar bears—need to live.

FAMOUS SKY WATCHERS

Swedish scientist Svante Arrhenius was the first to link growing levels of carbon dioxide in the atmosphere to global warming. He was awarded a Nobel Prize in Chemistry in 1903.

The Ozone Layer Is Becoming Thin

The ozone layer is a band of gas that sits in the stratosphere. It helps protect Earth from the Sun's UV rays. In the 1970s, scientists noticed that the ozone layer was becoming thin in places. Scientists believe this was caused by chemicals called chlorofluorocarbons, or CFCs, which escaped into the atmosphere.

Ⓥ Between 1981 and 1999, a large hole grew in the ozone above the Antarctic.

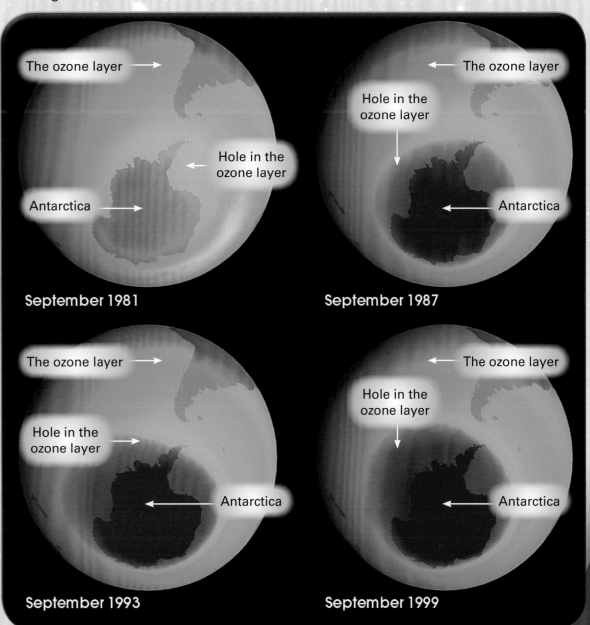

The ozone layer → ← The ozone layer

Hole in the ozone layer

Antarctica → ← Antarctica

September 1981   **September 1987**

The ozone layer → ← The ozone layer

Hole in the ozone layer

Antarctica   Antarctica

September 1993   **September 1999**

WHAT ARE THE BEST WAYS TO WATCH THE ATMOSPHERE?

The atmosphere is all around you and above you. Every time you look at the sky, you look at the atmosphere. The weather is what you see most often.

Weather Watching

Look at the sky and write down the time and what you see. Now look at the same part of the sky using binoculars or a telescope. Write down the time and what you can see now.

Satellite maps are also useful for weather watching. Look up a local weather site or national weather service site on the Internet. Find satellite maps for the time you looked at the weather.

How different are these views of the weather?

Useful Equipment for Backyard Weather Watching	
Equipment	**What It Is Used for**
Binoculars or a Telescope	A pair of binoculars or a telescope will help you see objects in the atmosphere in more detail.
Satellite Map	A satellite map will help you look at the weather in your area. Visit the website of your weather service for an updated map.
Compass	A compass will help you face the right direction when you are using the satellite maps.

Useful Websites

Greenhouse Effect: http://www.epa.gov/climatechange/kids/greenhouse.html

The Nine-Eyed MISR: http://spaceplace.nasa.gov/en/kids/misr_xword/misr_xword2.shtml

Satellite Images: http://www.weather.gov/sat_tab.php?image=ir

Scattering of Light: http://scifiles.larc.nasa.gov/text/kids/Problem_Board/problems/light/sim2.html

GLOSSARY

asteroids Small, rocky, or metal space objects that orbit the Sun.

atmosphere The layer of gases that surrounds a planet, moon, or star.

carbon dioxide An invisible gas that is produced when humans and animals breathe.

comets Small, rocky and icy space objects that have long, shining tails that are visible when orbiting near the Sun.

fossil fuels Substances that formed in the Earth's crust from the remains of plants and animals that lived millions of years ago, and which produce energy when burned (such as coal, oil, and natural gas).

gases Substances that are not solid or liquid, and are usually invisible.

gravitational pull The forces of gravity that attract two objects toward each other.

gravity The force that attracts all objects toward each other.

matter A substance of a particular kind, such as gas and dust.

meteoroids Small space objects that are made of rock and metal, ranging from several feet wide to the size of a pea.

nitrogen An invisible gas that makes up 78 percent of Earth's atmosphere.

orbit To travel around another, larger space object.

oxygen An invisible gas produced by plants that makes up about 20 percent of Earth's atmosphere and makes air breathable.

ozone layer A band of gas found within the stratosphere and which absorbs many of the Sun's harmful rays.

particles Very small parts of substances or matter.

radiation Energy that travels in the form of waves or rays and can be harmful to living things.

satellites Natural or human-made objects that orbit a planet.

solar system The Sun and everything that orbits it, including planets and other space objects.

space The area in which the solar system, stars, and galaxies exist, also known as the universe.

ultraviolet (UV) rays Invisible rays that are a part of sunlight and are harmful to human eyes and skin in large amounts.

water vapor Tiny particles of water that are no longer a liquid and can be carried in the air.

wavelength The waves in which light and sound travel; different types of sounds and colors have waves of different length.

INDEX